THE LIBRARY
ST. MARY'S COLLEGE OF MARYLAND
ST. MARY'S CITY, MARYLAND 20686

D1786779

'*THE MUSICAL PILGRIM*'

General Editor   Dr. Arthur Somervell

TCHAIKOVSKY
ORCHESTRAL WORKS

BY
ERIC BLOM

GREENWOOD PRESS, PUBLISHERS
WESTPORT, CONNECTICUT

Originally published in 1927
by Oxford University Press, London

First Greenwood Reprinting 1970

Library of Congress Catalogue Card Number 70-109711

SBN 8371-4202-4

Printed in the United States of America

FOREWORD

IN my original plan for this little book I made provision for an introductory chapter on the salient qualities and defects of Tchaikovsky's music. This seemed to be desirable, since the discussion of an arbitrary selection of only four of his works could hardly be expected to cover his art as a whole, although it will probably be conceded that the choice determined upon between the Editor, the Publishers, and myself has fallen upon compositions representative enough to expose the most characteristic aspects of his orchestral output. Keeping the chapter in question in reserve until the rest of my task was accomplished, I discovered that most of the points I had intended to raise therein already called for notice at various stages of the book and were sufficiently relevant to the works under review to fit in quite naturally with the context. I then decided that no purpose would be served in writing an introduction which could be little more than a summary of much that appears in the analytical chapters, and that I had better engage the reader's attention at once in the detailed discussion of the four works selected for investigation. A few remarks of a general nature which I had desired to make and which did not suggest themselves in the course of writing, I was subsequently able to incorporate here and there in the discourse without, I hope, making the intrusion too obvious.

E. B.

LONDON, *December* 1926.

CONTENTS

'Romeo and Juliet'	5
Piano Concerto No. 1, in B flat minor .	13
Symphony No. 4, in F minor . .	23
Suite from the Ballet 'Casse-Noisette' .	42

'Romeo and Juliet', Fantasy-Overture

Composed, Autumn 1869. Revised, Summer 1870.
Orchestration: Piccolo, 2 Flutes, 2 Oboes, English Horn, 2 Clarinets, 2 Bassoons, 4 Horns, 2 Trumpets, 3 Trombones, Tuba, Kettledrums, Bass Drum, Cymbals, Harp, and Strings.

The first of Tchaikovsky's works inspired by a Shakespearian subject,[1] the Fantasy-Overture on 'Romeo and Juliet', owes its existence to a suggestion of Mili Balakirev, with whom Tchaikovsky had some intercourse in the late eighteen-sixties, and who may have cherished the hope of winning him over to the Russian nationalist school. At Eastertide in 1868 Tchaikovsky paid a visit to St. Petersburg and for the first time came into contact with Balakirev, the leader of the group of patriot-musicians, as well as with Dargomijsky, Cui, Rimsky-Korsakov, and the critic Vladimir Stassov. The friendly relations which sprang up were not destined to ripen into a close association on Tchaikovsky's part with the ideals of the nationalists; but the antagonism was purely artistic and neither side ever allowed it to become personal, even when, later on, it occasionally resulted in some rather acrimonious mutual criticism. The fact that the association between the opponents soon ceased was due as much to geographical conditions as to the differences in their aesthetic outlook. Tchaikovsky lived alternately in Moscow, in the country, and abroad, while the 'Invincible Five' and their disciples had St. Petersburg for their centre.

Meanwhile Balakirev exercised a certain influence on

[1] The others are 'The Tempest', Symphony-Fantasia (Op. 18); 'Hamlet', Overture-Fantasia (Op. 67); Incidental Music to 'Hamlet' (Op. 67a); Vocal Duet from 'Romeo and Juliet'.

6 Orchestral Works of Tchaikovsky

Tchaikovsky. When the latter returned to Moscow in August 1869, after a visit to his sister, Alexandra Davidov, at Kamenka, he found Balakirev staying there in the company of Borodin. They met frequently and Balakirev suggested the composition of a work on the subject of 'Romeo and Juliet', which he felt to be admirably suited to his friend's temperament. He was himself an ardent Shakespearian and had composed an Overture and incidental music to 'King Lear' in 1861. His interest in the new work was so great that he discussed it in detail with Tchaikovsky, and went so far as to suggest, not only the general plan of the piece, but the character, *tempo*, and key of every section. About the end of October 1869 the Fantasy-Overture was finished and dedicated to Balakirev. But Tchaikovsky was not satisfied with it, and after its first performance, given in Moscow by Nicholas Rubinstein in March 1870, he made a thorough revision of it, which was completed the following summer.

It may have been Balakirev's criticism, tempered always by friendly interest, that induced the composer to take the work in hand a second time. Unfortunately his anxiety to destroy all traces of compositions he had once decided to regard as unworthy of him has deprived us, in this case as in many others, of the interesting study which never fails to arise from the privilege of a glimpse into an artist's workshop. We are told, for instance, that Tchaikovsky wrote the introductory section almost anew, but all we know about the original version is that Balakirev, who desired something in the nature of Liszt's chorales in the old Catholic Church style, thought the initial theme deficient in either strength or beauty, and resembling a passage from a Haydn quartet rather than an ecclesiastical melody.

'Romeo and Juliet', Fantasy-Overture

The new version opens with an unmistakable church theme, but it must be confessed that both in melody and harmony it is suggestive of the Russian Orthodox, not of the Roman, faith:

Ex. 1. *Andante non tanto, quasi moderato.*
Clarinets & Bassoons. *p* — *poco più f*

Perhaps this hardly matters, however, in connexion with Shakespeare, who himself did not hesitate to call an Athenian weaver and an Illyrian toper by such homespun English names as Bottom and Sir Toby Belch. What might be regarded as a more serious blemish is that the long introductory section, intended to represent Friar Laurence, lends an air of excessive importance to that minor character. Yet it will not do to base one's censure on Balakirev's suggestions rather than on what Tchaikovsky actually did with his music. Although the introduction extends to nearly a hundred bars of moderate *tempo*, it by no means depicts Friar Laurence throughout as an isolated personage, but hints at his relations with the protagonists. There is no doubt that the stabbing accents which start up one after another close upon the exposition of the ecclesiastical theme and the rising harp chords which follow, foreshadow the tragic passion of Romeo and Juliet, if only as perceived through the Friar's mind.

It lay in the comprehensive nature of Shakespeare's drama that a faithful delineation of the course it pursues could not be satisfactorily fitted in with the formal pattern of an overture, which demanded symphonic treatment with recurrent principal themes, working-out, recapitulation, and so on. Tchaikovsky must have been aware of these formal exigencies when he apologized with the additional title of 'Fantasy' for such deviations from the classical overture as he permitted himself. But he seems to have been unwilling to sacrifice it altogether, and thus it came about that certain incidents, such as the street brawls between the retainers of the Montagues and Capulets assume a thematic significance in the music which is utterly disproportionate to their importance in the drama. Tchaikovsky laboured under peculiar difficulties, imposed by the subject of his choice, which does not happen to bend itself so happily to the despotism of an established musical form as some of Strauss's literary topics did.[1] He had to select his symphonic themes from a multitude of dramatic incidents, and was bound to leave their exact meaning rather indeterminate.

The musical transition from the introduction to the dramatic centre is a superb piece of stage-management. After a dialogue of suspensions accompanied by passages in thirds that creep up and down with the effect of an organ playing on soft reed stops, the church theme returns to running *pizzicato* figures. Suddenly there is an ominous drum roll and the sharp accents are roused again by a swift stirring of the rhythmic pulse; the liturgical theme itself is swept into the growing excitement. By a touch of genius Tchaikovsky, instead of coining new material for this precipitation into action, merely dramatizes what he had already introduced, thus giving the hearer the sensation of watching familiar figures fatally drawn into a whirlpool of tragedy.

[1] It was almost inevitable that the adventures of Don Juan and of Till Eulenspiegel should take the Rondo form and those of Don Quixote be represented by variations.

'Romeo and Juliet', Fantasy-Overture

The incident of the street brawl begins in this manner:

Ex. 2. *Allegro giusto.*

Musically, this is the first principal subject, while the tumult with which Shakespeare begins is nothing more than, as it were, a key-signature. We must therefore take refuge in the indefiniteness of musical illustration and accept this theme, which occupies a good deal of the formal development of the Overture, as typifying not only the snarling and biting of thumbs of the retainers of the two estranged families, but the feud of their houses in its general consequences. The broken rhythms, clamorous orchestration, and the confusion of the scale passages in the strings suggest hatred and strife admirably. As the exposition proceeds, the following curious rhythm, which sounds like the clanging together of swords wielded with uncontrolled fury, arrests attention:

Ex. 3.
Allegro.

Soon afterwards the uproar dies down, and as its last echoes seem to reverberate along the alleys of Verona, the love theme is given out by English horn and muted violas to syncopated horn chords and a soft *pizzicato* bass. It is one of the finest inspirations even of so exceptional a melody-maker as it must be admitted Tchaikovsky was, whatever else may be found wanting in his art. On its first appearance this tune is comparatively brief:

but already it has an aching intensity that at once grips the hearer's imagination. But when, later on, it returns, greatly extended by ever-new turns of dolorous ecstasy, in the flutes and oboes, and is accompanied by a moaning horn figure, it acquires a plaintive beauty that all but matches Shakespeare in poignancy. In the meantime a new idea arises from the muted violins:

This is sometimes described as a second love theme, but its tranquil loveliness may well be accepted as a premonition of the lovers' death—the only peace that is to be theirs. Balakirev thought it expressed to perfection the sweetness, tenderness, and longing of love;

'Romeo and Juliet', Fantasy-Overture

the only reproach he had to level at it was that it lacked spirituality, a criticism that is hardly justified, for Romeo and Juliet, absorbed by each other and enwrapped in their passion, scarcely possess that quality.

A tranquil connecting passage with a conspicuous harp part leads to the working-out section, which combines the theme of Friar Laurence with those of the feud with no dramatic justification, unless one cared to indulge in subtleties of interpretation which were probably far from the composer's mind. He merely found that the two themes went well together and sacrificed literary reasoning to formal ingenuity. We here find Tchaikovsky following the method adopted by Weber in his Overtures, which do not attempt to tell the stories of the Operas to which they belong, but simply weld the chief thematic ideas into a symphonic movement. The justification of such a procedure is to be measured by nothing but its *musical* result, which is after all the main consideration that should govern a musical work. An even more drastic, yet no less successful, musical inflation of an unimportant incident in the same drama was committed by Berlioz, who made a whole symphonic piece out of the few lines of poetical imagery relating to Queen Mab.

Sinister chords, heard alternately in brass and woodwind to a violin note repeated in syncopation, are a remarkable feature of the working-out:

The so-called second love theme (No. 5) returns next, now played by the wind to a murmuring violin accompaniment that suggests the consciousness of enmity which obsesses the minds of the ill-fated pair. Then, with a fine upward sweep, comes a passionate outpouring of the great love melody (No. 4), set against quivering triplets. For a moment it begins to droop and then it flows forth once more, rudely interrupted by the brawl theme (No. 2), against which it is powerless. Neither can that of Friar Laurence (No. 1), sounded forcibly by the brass, withstand this storm of hate. When the music sinks down at last, the love melody is heard, broken and gasping, to a rigidly repeated drum figure. Solemn, sustained harmonies in the wood-wind and brass are answered by the rising harp chords of the introduction, which accompany a last soaring upward of the love song. The silence is rent by a violent broken rhythm akin to No. 3, which seemed out of place to some of Tchaikovsky's friends: it is nothing of the kind, for although the tragedy ends with the reconciliation of the afflicted enemies, it is their hate that was its dominant motive. It is, moreover, characteristic of Tchaikovsky to finish with a somewhat lurid touch of drama. Great showman that he was, he could not drop the curtain quietly on the lovers' death; he must needs conclude by audibly knocking the nails into their coffin. This insistent manner of making our flesh creep to the last may be vulgar, but it must be accepted as a sincere form of self-expression.

Piano Concerto No. 1, in B flat minor (Op. 23)

Composed, November 1874—February 1875. Revised, 1889.
Orchestration: Solo Piano, 2 Flutes, 2 Oboes, 2 Clarinets, 2 Bassoons, 4 Horns, 2 Trumpets, 3 Trombones, Kettledrums, and Strings.

1. Allegro non troppo e molto maestoso.—Allegro con spirito. 2. Andantino semplice—Prestissimo.—Tempo I. 3. Allegro con fuoco.

THERE are few works, probably, of which musicians are more weary than the first of Tchaikovsky's three piano Concertos, the only one that is ever played, and played to excess. It may be that a literary discussion of a piece so staled by custom may only make the surfeit more unendurable, but since it is a question here of singling out a handful of typical works in order to study the most characteristic aspects of Tchaikovsky's art, the omission of so representative a specimen as this Concerto could hardly be justified. Besides, it must not be forgotten that its greatest fault, lack of freshness, is after all the result of merits great enough to have secured it the universal currency of which it is now showing the wear. Between ourselves and Tchaikovsky—for we have nothing to do here with the guilty pianistic intermediary—the Concerto remains an achievement which, due allowance made for divergence of taste, can never be regarded as negligible.

The most striking of the qualities that distinguish the Concerto from any other work written for piano and orchestra is a peculiar flavour that is due, first of all, to the singular turn of Tchaikovsky's thematic invention, and secondly to a technique of keyboard writing that is his own secret, or, if one will, one of his failings. Compared with that of Chopin, Schumann, or

Liszt, his pianistic style is certainly not ideal. The soloist is here and there confronted with difficulties which, though not greater than those encountered in many another Concerto, are less justified by the resulting effect. In the introduction, for example, some of the octave passages are made much harder to play by the insertion of chordal notes which yield no additional beauty or power; if anything, they reduce the mordant brilliance of these vigorously hammered figures by diverting some of the energy of the impact from the extreme notes.

Tchaikovsky himself admitted that he found the invention of pianistic passages rather troublesome, thus accounting for the comparatively long time he spent on the composition of the Concerto. We cannot tell how far the original version may have been deficient in the matter of pianism, since only the composer's revision, made fourteen years later, is now extant. All we know is that so great an authority as Nicholas Rubinstein was dissatisfied with the work, and unfortunately said so bluntly enough to rouse an obstinate resolution in Tchaikovsky not to alter a note, when milder and less exaggerated criticism might have had the opposite effect. The composer, in high dudgeon, erased the inscription of Rubinstein's name on his score and dedicated the work to Hans von Bülow, who introduced it to American audiences before it was heard in Russia. Tchaikovsky and Rubinstein later met halfway in their estimation of it: the former admitted its defects readily enough to re-write it, the latter recognized its merits and took it into his repertory. The first to play it in Russia, however, was Taneiev, who made his first appearance with it in Moscow on 21 November/3 December 1875.

Piano Concerto No. 1, in B flat minor

I. There is a broad introduction that has a melody of its own:

Ex. 7.

an expansive tune such as only an inexhaustible melodist like Tchaikovsky could afford to lavish on a preliminary section and then drop without any further reference. Admirable though this fertility may be, it is not without its disadvantages. By the time the exposition of the true thematic material is reached, this song has become so significant that any hearer who is unacquainted with the Concerto must inevitably, though perhaps unconsciously, expect it to return somewhere or other before the work is over. There is a vague feeling of a formal blemish, a lack of balance; it is as if a character in the prologue to a play had given the impression of being the hero of the drama and was then simply discarded by the author without any explanation. A composer must sometimes know how to create music that is merely background, how to establish a mood without at once engaging the listener's whole imagination.

Crashing, far-flung chords sweep like dashing waves around this firm melody. Then, after a rather precocious cadenza, the rhythm is tightened by the placing of thematic fragments closer together within the bars, with the result that the accents are displaced and a feeling of precipitation is conveyed. In the art of arousing expectation Tchaikovsky has no superiors. The fulfilment comes with a last return of the sweeping melody, accompanied by rhythmically repeated chords in the piano part. The tune then sinks down, the music becomes hushed and expectant, distant trumpet calls announce some tremendous musical event.

What actually does occur is a change to *allegro con spirito* and the introduction of this paltry first subject:

Ex. 8. *Allegro con spirito.*
Pfte. in octaves.

It is said to be a Malo-Russian song which Tchaikovsky heard sung by blind beggars. If that be so, he must surely have modified it considerably, for it is quite inconceivable that it could have been sung as it stands even by a beggar, so destitute is it of melodic quality. As it prances on there is what Tchaikovsky himself described as a duel rather than a duet between the piano and the orchestra. The treatment of this poor principal subject, it must be conceded, is highly original, and the rattling passages in broken threefold octaves are an interesting specimen of Tchaikovsky's individual handling of the pianistic idiom.

Excellent, too, are the tentative allusions to the second subject which occur twice before the first is dismissed. The more happily invented new theme again demonstrates Tchaikovsky's melodic gift, which is not merely a matter of curving and measuring his notes into a distinctive phrase, but a knack of extending

Piano Concerto No. 1, in B flat minor

the passage at its repetition and bending it into a new shape. The second subject opens thus:

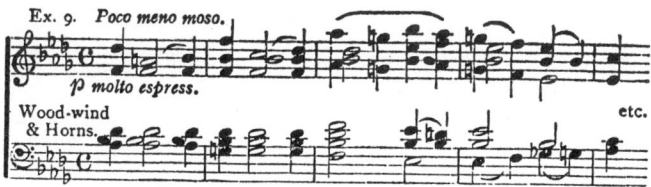

As if this were not sufficient luxuriance to oppose to the arid first subject, he must needs give us a complementary phrase, shorter and simpler, but no less cunningly devised to cling to the memory than No. 9:

Very curious is the displacement of the melodic accent by half a bar, for the ear cannot escape the impression that it sounds as follows:

while to watch the conductor for guidance as to its proper position is only to be confused by his beat. The phrases of the true second subject (No. 9), which the pianist scatters lightly into this theme, have a charming effect in their new presentation, embedded in arpeggios.

The bald patch of brilliant irrelevance which follows is an oratorical error of the first magnitude. As regards sonority, this passage is a climax, that is to say, one of those points where the subject-matter ought to be delivered with the fullest weight of argument, but as it is devoid of ideas, it gives one the uncomfortable feeling of being compelled to listen to mere verbose gush. It is in episodes of this kind that Tchaikovsky, though persuasive enough, fails utterly to be impressive.

The passage having petered out in an arpeggio, there is an unexpected return of the auxiliary melody of the second subject, now actually written as it sounds (No. 11). It creeps in quietly on the muted strings and marks the beginning of a working-out section evolved by re-statement of the thematic material in new ways rather than by its organic growth, but at any rate formally satisfying until once more the music loses itself in a merely rhetorical climax. It is saved, however, by the return of the second subject (No. 9), which now really achieves something of a true development. It leads back to the principal theme (No. 8) and through it, by a short cut, to a condensed recapitulation that pulls the music together quite satisfactorily, although the second subject is treated at excessive length in comparison with the first. Tchaikovsky unconsciously tries to atone in this way for his unhappy choice of a main theme, but cannot reconcile the deservedly short shrift he now gives it with ideal balance of form. The enormous and very difficult cadenza, which was fully written out by the composer, is likewise based on No. 9. A brilliant *coda* intensifies and speeds up the preceding material into a few final pages which seem new, but are organically connected with what went before.

II. There is a curiously incongruous phrase at the opening of the slow movement, where the flute has this figure in the score:

Piano Concerto No. 1, in B flat minor 19

Ex. 12. *Andantino semplice.*

Fl. *p dolcissimo.*

Throughout the movement this principal theme subsequently appears thus:

Ex. 13,

a fact which has induced most conductors to change the F in the first bar of the flute passage to the B flat above. Nothing, certainly, can reconcile the printed version of this passage with the later form of the theme, but it leads to some interesting speculations. It may be merely a printer's error, but it may also afford some insight into Tchaikovsky's melody-making, if one assumes that he only hit upon the second and more distinctive turn of the phrase in the course of composition and forgot to alter the first statement of his theme already written down. This would argue a high degree of subtlety in his perception of the finer inflexions of a tune, for there is no doubt that the first phrase quoted above is flat and indefinite, whereas the little lift given to it later at once imparts plasticity and precision to it. It is just that little upturned hook into which it is bent that makes it catch on to one's memory and stay there.

A second phrase, light and fantastic, is of some structural importance:

Ex. 14. *Andantino.*

Pfte. *p*

It is the one feature, in fact, that does something to weld this lyrical section to the frivolous *prestissimo*—a kind of *scherzando* middle section—where the orchestra sings a little French *chansonette* while the soloist is busy with rapid passage work. The French song is said to be a reminiscence of Désirée Artôt, the famous singer to whom Tchaikovsky became engaged in 1868, but who soon afterwards married the baritone Padilla. It began with the words, 'Il faut s'amuser, danser et rire,' and opens in this manner on the violas and violoncellos:

There is no denying the force of the injunction that one must be amused, dance, and laugh, but it is a little difficult to see the necessity of doing so in the middle of the slow movement of a Concerto. We have here a glaring instance of Tchaikovsky's inveterate selfishness: even in a work that has so far been mainly decorative and certainly nowhere expressive of personal emotion, he cannot refrain from introducing some intimate concern of his own and trying to interest us in it.

III. The Finale shows that Tchaikovsky was by no means averse to exploiting what the group of Russian nationalist composers had to teach, although he had no desire to limit himself by subscribing to their exclusive patriotic doctrine.[1] He was by disposition and education a composer who wished to be unhampered: an artist first and a Russian only afterwards. The 'Invincible Five' and their adherents, on the other hand, were

---

[1] Tchaikovsky's most consistently national work is the second Symphony (Op. 17) on Little-Russian themes.

Piano Concerto No. 1, in B flat minor

Russian artists or nothing. To tax Tchaikovsky with Italianism, as is often done, is, to say the least, thoughtless, for the Italians of his time were themselves not consciously Italian in their music. If he resembled them at all, it was by a certain temperamental affinity, not by a voluntary act of artistic expatriation. They were exuberant melodists: so was he; they had no use for counterpoint: neither had he; to apply learning to music for its own sake as the Germans did, or craft as the Frenchmen did, was neither for them nor for him; both factors were of use only in so far as they went to the making of music that should either give delight or express emotion. Like many of them, he was a hedonist even when he indulged in self-pity: his affliction was that of not being able to take pleasure, and give it, indefinitely. Hence the lack of depth in his pessimism, the want of elevation in his tragic moods.

The first subject of the Finale is in the style of a Cossack dance:

Its biting, rather savage rhythm is intensified a little later on when the $\frac{3}{4}$ time of the piano part is set against a $\frac{6}{8}$ effect in the orchestra. The second subject is energetically given out by the full orchestra:

Ex. 17. Allegro. Full Orch. etc.

and repeated, *poco meno mosso*, by the soloist with characteristic imitations in the nature of a duet between two voices, male and female. A broad third theme follows immediately:

Ex. 18. Poco meno mosso. Vlns. 1 & 2.

Here we have the perfect expression of a Slav with a cosmopolitan culture. The melody is Russian without a doubt, yet not a Russian national tune. Such folk elements as cling to it are perfumed by the balladry of fashionable drawing-rooms; it mirrors the affectations of rusticity among a society which still speaks French in preference to the vernacular, considered too rude an idiom for polite occasions. Tchaikovsky often falls into this would-be homely language with a foreign drawl to it, especially in his songs, and it is this sort of thing in his music that must have made the nationalists see red.

The piano repeats this theme in a manner that shows Tchaikovsky's happy way of sustaining the hearer's interest by extension and slight variation. The section marked *sostenuto molto*, which stands for the working-out, makes much of figures of this type:

Ex. 19. Sostenuto molto. Vlns. 1.

Piano Concerto No. 1, in B flat minor

with which fragments of the main theme are combined. The material is then passed in review again by way of recapitulation with the customary changes of key.

In a *molto più mosso*, where the music now palpably heads towards the close, both Nos. 16 and 18 are used in a new way. At the return of the initial *tempo* occurs a passage where Tchaikovsky, beginning quietly with allusions to various themes, works up one of those gradual *crescendi*, those cumulative climaxes, which by their growing force and eloquence seem to pull a whole movement together and compel one to become aware of its coherence. The passage in question begins purely orchestrally, but the soloist suddenly enters imperiously with thundering octave scales. They make a great deal of themselves, yet mean so little that they threaten to wreck the whole powerful peroration; but just in time a vigorous outburst of No. 18, piano and all, impressively broadened out and once more taking an unexpected shape, saves the situation and leads quite naturally to the flamboyant conclusion.

Symphony No. 4, in F minor (Op. 36)

Composed, April 1877—January 1878.
Orchestration: Piccolo, 2 Flutes, 2 Oboes, 2 Clarinets, 2 Bassoons, 4 Horns, 2 Trumpets, 3 Trombones, Tuba, Kettledrums, Bass Drum, Cymbals, Triangle, and Strings.

1. Andante sostenuto—Moderato con anima. 2. Andantino in modo di canzone. 3. Scherzo: Allegro. 4. Allegro con fuoco.

THE fourth Symphony being largely an autobiographical work, it is important to know as much of its genesis as possible. A great deal of mystery still enshrouds the story of Tchaikovsky's unhappy marriage, with which this work coincides; his biographers so far have been so tactful that only with the aid of conjecture and imaginative reconstruction of the psychological aspects of this painful episode is it possible to come to anything like a definite conclusion. But until inference is supported by documentary evidence—which may perhaps never be forthcoming—no purpose is served by recording such personal conclusions as one may have formed from the known facts of the case.

The plain truth, so far as it is known, is this: In April 1877 Tchaikovsky suffered from an acute fit of mental depression, produced, it seems, by his duties at the Moscow Conservatoire, which he found extremely irksome. Although he had already received a communication from his future benefactress, Nadejda von Meck, who had ordered some arrangements for violin and piano of several of his works on such fantastically high terms that the commission could only be regarded as charity in disguise, he did not yet see his way to relinquish his professorial duties and devote himself entirely to creative work. Such were the conditions in which he began the composition of the fourth Symphony. At the end of May he was engaged to Antonina Ivanovna Miliukov, from whom he had received the declaration of a despairing love, the kind of fierce devotion that borders on madness and death. He did not reciprocate these feelings in the least, but touched by their passionate sincerity and moved by who knows what emotions of pity and chivalry, anxious too, perhaps, to have a peaceful home of his own, he allowed himself to be rushed into a disastrous marriage. The wedding took place on 6/18 July. Twenty days later the composer left for Kamenka, driven to despair by an irresistible

Symphony No. 4, in F minor (Op. 36)

aversion to his wife, which he may have attributed to his nervous condition and hoped to overcome in the country. He found enough calm there to continue working at the Symphony during August, and in September he returned home to Moscow. By 24 September/6 October the drama had reached its culminating point. Tchaikovsky suddenly left for St. Petersburg in a state of frenzy verging on lunacy. After a violent nervous crisis his doctor declared that only a complete change of life and surroundings could save him from disaster. A separation from his wife for good and all was unavoidable.

In October Tchaikovsky left for Switzerland in the company of his brother Anatol. He enjoyed a period of rest at Clarens, on the Lake of Geneva. He was short of money, but a letter from Nadejda von Meck—whom he had not met and was destined never to know personally—came with the timely offer of an annuity of 6,000 roubles. Early in November he went to Italy, visiting Milan, Florence, Rome, and Venice. It was at the latter place that, after a brief excursion to Vienna, he completed the fourth Symphony in December. Only the finishing touches of the orchestration were missing, and these Tchaikovsky added in January 1878, during a sojourn at San Remo, where he also completed the Opera, 'Eugene Onegin'. The Symphony was dedicated 'to my best friend'—needless to say, Nadejda von Meck. On 10/22 February, while Tchaikovsky was still in Italy, the first performance was given by the Russian Musical Society in Moscow.

Tchaikovsky is much criticized for the self-centred nature of many of his works, and the criticism is well founded, so long as the view that it is not a composer's business to commit his personal affairs to paper for the edification of the world can be logically defended. Theoretically the objection to such a motive of creation is certainly justified, but there are practical exceptions, of which Tchaikovsky is unquestionably one. For it cannot be denied that the impulse to write some of his strongest and most characteristic music is only to be attributed to intimate experiences, to struggles and tragedies which more than once produced in him a state of acute neurosis that involved his whole being in a state of overwrought excitability alternating with utter prostration. That this condition actively affected his creative faculty and let it burn with an especially ardent flame, happened to be one of its pathological phenomena, probably—if one may venture on the hypothesis—the one that saved him from irremediable mental collapse.

If we are to condemn a work of art inspired by personal experiences, neither the sonnets of Petrarch and Shakespeare, nor the Monna Lisa of Leonardo, nor yet Wagner's 'Tristan und Isolde' can be accepted as the masterpieces they in fact are. Criticism, to be quite honest with itself, will have to recognize that Tchaikovsky's fourth Symphony is not imperfect because it is biographical or subjective or whatever else one may care to call it, but because it is not absolutely great *qua* biographical or subjective music. What is wrong with it is a matter, not of kind, but of degree: it is not the product of a soul shaken to its depths, but only of a pathological state, a nerve crisis.

Nevertheless, taken on its own terms, it expresses more perfectly than the music of any other composer the despair and self-pity of an artist's mind wrought up to the point of delirium. All that militates against its being positively great is the fact that suffering which

Symphony No. 4, in F minor (Op. 36)

is in its essence largely physical has no chance of making a universal appeal. Great agonies of the heart, the strife and distress of an intellect, expressed in terms of art find their echo in mankind at large because they are, like art itself, removed from the material plane; physical pain, even in its mental results, is too personally confined to win more than sympathy: it cannot be shared by others to the extent of being felt actively, and not merely by reflection. Tchaikovsky, therefore, where he gives vent to material suffering, as in the present Symphony or in the 'Pathetic', frets rather than moves us and tempers the sympathy he awakens with something like disdain. But that he pleads his cause with the eloquent conviction of the complete egotist cannot be disputed.

I. Tchaikovsky openly confessed that this work of his was indebted to Beethoven's fifth Symphony. Like that masterpiece, his fourth Symphony has for its central idea a theme of Fate. The composer was himself fully aware that he was not a second Beethoven, and he acknowledged his inferiority as frankly as his indebtedness. All the same, the manner in which he begins this Symphony holds out the highest promise. Compared with the peremptory, heart-shaking rap of Beethoven, the more circumstantial knocking at the door of Tchaikovsky's Fate theme is apt to quicken one's breath to an expectant panting rather than to cut it off for an awestruck moment; but about its impressiveness, as it stands there stark and bare of all harmony, there can be no two opinions:

Ex. 20. *Andante sostenuto.*
Bsns. & Hns.

What follows in the short *andante* introduction that prefaces the Symphony even reinforces the chilling effect produced on our senses. The changing harmonies which now begin to grope under the motif just quoted and continue, as it were, to seek the right key to some mystery, seem to portend a tremendous tragedy:

Ex. 21. Andante.
W.-wind *ff* & Brass.

But, as in the piano Concerto, the fulfilment falls greatly short of the prophecy, for what do we find as the symphonic movement actually begins? A waltz. It is, truth to tell, not by any means a gay or frivolous waltz, for it has a hectic flush about it, and the irregular rhythmic pulse that accompanies it suggests the throbbing of a heart in despair (Ex. 22).

The music conveys scarcely more than the private distresses of a ballet girl; yet, to infuse so much tragic horror into a dance measure is an achievement scarcely equalled elsewhere in music. Verdi alone, perhaps, could do it, and even he only with the aid of a stage situation that was in itself affecting.

The orchestra paints in crude colours. The strings fling out their phrases with many agitated scales and

Symphony No. 4, in F minor (Op. 36)

Ex. 22. *Moderato con anima.*

tremolos, the wood-wind accentuates sharply, the horns cry out anguish in passages that move up and down in semitones. At last the ground-swell of passionate agony breaks upon the crest of a climax, and in the silence is heard a little pathetic dialogue between clarinet and bassoon. The musical pulse halts and slackens, and now the clarinet introduces the second subject, a daintily tripping figure, but not without a kind of strangled utterance of sorrow:

Ex. 23. *Moderato assai, quasi andante.*

It is doubtless the 'pathetic effort to forget' mentioned by Tchaikovsky in the programme he outlined for Nadejda von Meck. The little derisive group of notes that follows (bar 3 of No. 23) is scattered up and down the woodwind. Then comes a counter-melody in the violoncellos that must be regarded as part of the second subject:

Ex. 24. *Moderato assai.*

a rather unctuous tune of the kind that insinuates itself somewhere or other into almost every orchestral work of Tchaikovsky's, and is as a matter of course given to the most lachrymose instrument in the orchestra. It is in connexion with this part of the movement that Tchaikovsky says in his note: 'Is it not better to turn from reality and lose ourselves in dreams? . . . O joy! A sweet and tender dream enfolds me. A bright and serene presence leads me on.'

Flutes and oboes repeat No. 24, the counterpoint (No. 23) always teasing and chuckling gracefully. More warmly, the violins now embrace the second subject (fragments of Nos. 23 and 24), while the wood-wind, very quietly, suggests the principal theme (No. 22), like the presence of some impending unrest somewhere in the background. But it comes quickly to the fore, and the two main themes are no longer confined to separate instrumental groups. They begin to wrestle for supremacy and the struggle grows more and more desperate. The first subject imposes its quicker *tempo* and soon has the upper hand, being given out with greater force and more stressful accentuation than before. Suddenly, it seems to cower as before a blow, and then, with a crashing drum roll, the Fate motif (No. 20) is hurled out by the trumpets. 'This is fate,' says Tchaikovsky,

—that inevitable force which checks our aspirations towards happiness ere they reach their goal; which watches jealously lest our peace and bliss should be complete and cloudless—a force which, like the sword of Damocles, hangs perpetually over our heads and is always embittering the soul. This force is inescapable and invincible. There is no other course but to submit and inwardly lament.

The reappearance of No. 20 is the signal for the recapitulation, a formal feature which here quite natur-

Symphony No. 4, in F minor (Op. 36)   31

ally conforms to the programme, for as Fate reminds us that for all our dreams and fancies life must take its pre-ordained course, so the motto theme ushers in the return of the material heard in the exposition. Tchaikovsky by no means simply restates that section in its original form, but fashions the music anew and produces a feeling of organic growth by actually interweaving the Fate theme here and there with the principal subject (No. 22). The second subject returns with its first strain (No. 23) introduced by solo bassoon, while the second (No. 24) is given to solo horn. Again the conflict between the two themes begins, but it is cut short this time. Fate intervenes more insistently than ever, and in a precipitate peroration the theme associated with it (No. 20) remains victorious.

II. 'The second movement', in Tchaikovsky's own description,[1]

expresses another phase of suffering. Now it is the melancholy which steals over us when at evening we sit indoors alone, weary of work, while the book we have picked up for relaxation slips unheeded from our fingers. A long procession of old memories goes by. How sad to think how much is already past and gone! And yet these recollections of youth are sweet. We regret the past, although we have neither courage nor desire to start a new life. We are rather weary of existence. We would fain rest awhile and look back, recalling many things. There were moments when young blood pulsed through our veins and life gave all we asked. There were also moments of sorrow, irreparable loss. All this has receded so far into the past. How sad, yet sweet, to lose ourselves therein!

Tchaikovsky, it will be gathered from this, did not believe in the absolute contrasts that were essential to the classical symphony up to Beethoven's 'Eroica'—or perhaps better, up to Mozart's last three Symphonies,

[1] The translation used here and elsewhere is by Mrs. Rosa Newmarch.

each of which is certainly steeped in an atmosphere sufficiently unified to argue, if not a programme, at any rate a definite emotional impulse of creation. Tchaikovsky aimed at sharp contrasts indeed, but they were merely different aspects of one and the same underlying psychic state. He was so deeply immersed in the personal problems that troubled him at the time of writing such a work as the fourth Symphony, that he was perhaps hardly conscious of imparting to it the curious emotional coherence that is one of the outstanding qualities of his music at its best. It would be a fascinating task for the critic to determine what great factors in art are due to a kind of sublime accident and what to personal responsibility on the creator's part. Were this possible, it would lead to a fresh assessment of a good many values appraised by common consent rather than by individual judgement; but since it is not feasible, except in cases where the artist's own confessions are preserved for us, we must be content to accept art's lucky throws with the same amount of appreciation as its consciously attained successes.

The gentle song of the oboe with which the second movement opens, *andantino in modo di canzone*—a good example of a long-drawn and shapely melody in the best Tchaikovskian manner—though in the gloomy key of B flat minor, is wistful rather than sorrow-laden:

Ex. 25. *Andantino in modo di canzone.*

Ob. *p semplice ma grazioso.*

But on its repetition by the violoncellos it is already

Symphony No. 4, in F minor (Op. 36)

overshadowed by an ominous clarinet figure, darkly harmonized by horns and bassoons. A second strain:

Ex. 26. Andantino.

increases the emotional tension, which becomes greater at each of the swift and drastic modulations this theme undergoes four times in succession at a distance of only two bars:

Ex. 27. Andantino.

This passage may be singled out as a remarkable instance of Tchaikovsky's infallible feeling for the right harmonic colour with which to match a melodic idea. Any of the numerous striking tunes in which his work abounds, once heard, can never be detached in one's memory from the harmony that not merely accompanies it, but is actually an inseparable part of it.

There is no doubt that the invention of a theme simultaneously started in his mind the only sequence of chords that could possibly go with it in the particular turn his imagination took at the moment. Hence, to modify a melody once fixed was to give it immediately a different harmonic bearing. In the present instance, he not only thought of giving his theme that sudden upward lift which is in itself a happy discovery, but the idea inevitably drew after it the arresting excursions into remote keys, and these in turn suggested a climax. This is very brief, but it does not pass without leaving behind it the semiquaver motion it engendered as a new accompaniment to the initial theme (No. 25), now assigned to different instruments. Just as we seem to be reaching the same climax again and begin to wonder how the composer is to find a way out of an everlasting round of the same musical occurrences, a little insignificant rhythmic figure springs from the flutes. It is seized upon by the first clarinet, first horn, violas, and violoncellos in turn, consolidating the slight impression it made at first by insistent reiteration, until it has grown strong enough to establish its position as the principal theme of a new and more animated section, a kind of *trio*, in F major. The new theme is first stated in its definite form by clarinets and bassoons in octaves (Ex. 28). As it passes into the strings a counter-melody is added by the wood-wind, and afterwards the position is reversed. But Tchaikovsky, a melodist and harmonist second to none, was a poor contrapuntist. The additional theme, of course, fits in perfectly with its companion, but the very act of being so accommodating deprives it of any individuality of its own. Played by itself, it is a weak, lifeless thing. As the music grows more strenuous, triplet ornamentation imparts to it

Symphony No. 4, in F minor (*Op.* 36)

Ex. 28.

a rather artificial animation, but its rival is soon victorious in the unequal struggle.

The return of the principal section brings the theme No. 25 back in the first violins. Gliding figures in the wood-wind akin to those accompanying the second subject in the first movement (No. 23, bar 3) are a new feature. Whether they are pure ornamentation or have the significance of a 'leading motif' must remain open to conjecture. Composers sometimes receive credit for subtleties which they may never have intended. To Mozart, for instance, has been ascribed a good deal of ingenuity in making use of certain thematic formations in his Operas, especially 'The Magic Flute', in various recognizable forms to express analogous ideas. The probability is that nobody could be more astonished at these discoveries than Mozart would have been himself; but such strokes of genius, provided that they really exist and are not merely the invention of a commentator, are none the less admirable for being unconsciously brought off. Perhaps they are more so, since conscious contrivance argues talent and inspiration of which the creator is unaware—genius. The little touches of mockery which Tchaikovsky adds to the recurrence of a theme expressive of melancholy contémplation may be simply accepted for what they are worth, whether they be meant to convey any such idea or not. The second theme (No. 26) returns in its earlier form, but curtailed. The startling modulations (No. 27) are not used again, perhaps because a telling effect is inevitably weakened by repetition, perhaps only because a new turn has now to be found to lead the music to its conclusion. It is the principal theme, broken up into fragments, which provides the material for a quietly sorrowful *coda*. The only new feature is a long, drooping melodic line for the violoncellos.

III. The Scherzo is labelled *pizzicato ostinato*. All the string players lay their bows aside and pluck their instruments throughout this movement. The effect is not unlike that of a Russian *balalaïka* band, and, indeed, from Tchaikovsky's description one gathers that he had something of the sort in his mind, although it is hard to escape the feeling that he was not very clear about his own intentions. His explanation does not ring sincere: having once said that the Symphony had a programme, this movement, which was in reality absolute music, had somehow to be fitted with a description. Here it is:

> In the third movement no definite feelings find expression. Here we have only capricious arabesques, intangible forms, which come into a man's head when he has been drinking wine and his nerves are rather excited. His mood is neither joyful nor sad. He thinks of nothing in particular. His fancy is free to follow its own flight, and it designs the strangest patterns. Suddenly memory calls up the picture of a tipsy peasant and a street song. From afar come the sounds of a military band. These are the kind of confused images which pass through our brain as we fall asleep. They have no connexion with actuality, but are simply wild, strange, and bizarre.

Symphony No. 4, in F minor (Op. 36)

To this one must object that if a symphonic movement is to be expressive of nothing in particular, the introduction of a drunken peasant is scarcely defensible; also that a street song is something more than a capricious arabesque and a military band anything but an intangible form. The truth is that a charming piece of 'objective' music has been artificially burdened with a 'subjective' interpretation that is plainly an afterthought. It is in such cases that one deplores the egotistic bent in Tchaikovsky, which, even when he loses himself in his art, will not let him be content with the ability to forget.

The Scherzo begins with this theme, for *pizzicato* strings only:

The speed verges on the utmost that is possible to perform on plucked strings without disaster, but the dry, snappy tone imparts an extraordinary vitality to an otherwise rather undistinguished subject. The continuation is made still more piquant by syncopation, and the music swings neatly through its modulations before it reaches the opening bars again. By a similar process a *meno mosso* section is reached, where for the first time in this movement the wood-wind comes into play. Oboes and bassoons introduce the following new theme:

Ex. 30.

—too elegant an idea to represent a rustic toper or even a street song. The whole section, carried on by simple repetition over a drone bass, is scored for wood-wind only, while the next, which returns to the original *tempo*, is given to brass and drums alone. Its *staccato* theme, closely related to No. 29:

Ex. 31.

played very faintly, doubtless suggested the afterthought of the military band. That Tchaikovsky's mental process in the act of composition involved no such idea seems pretty clear when it is considered that the use of the brass alone was simply determined by the previous idea of writing alternately for the strings and wood-wind groups. The latter family soon joins into the *staccato* figures with fragments of Nos. 29 and 30, and the strings also make tentative entries that lead to the return of the initial material, at first stated as before. Later on No. 29 is bandied about between

Symphony No. 4, in F minor (Op. 36)

wood-wind and strings, and No. 30 returns in a new, breathless manner. A climax is built up and the music afterwards dies away in scattered thematic fragments.

IV. The Finale is decidedly inferior to the rest of the Symphony. That it makes a brilliant climax cannot be denied, but the heightening of the effect is gained by greater dynamic intensity—the scoring in fact is rather blatant—not by any elevation of tone. In spite of this, Tchaikovsky ascribes the mission of a kind of moral summary to this last movement:

> 'If you can find', he says, 'no reason for happiness in yourself, look at others. Go to the people. See how they can enjoy life and give themselves up entirely to festivity. A rustic holiday is depicted. Hardly have we had time to forget ourselves in the spectacle of other people's pleasure, when indefatigable Fate reminds us once more of its presence. Others pay no heed to us. They do not spare us a glance, nor stop to observe that we are lonely and sad. How merry, how glad they all are! All their feelings are so inconsequent, so simple. And will you still say that all the world is immersed in sorrow? Happiness does exist, simple and unspoilt. Be glad in other's gladness. This makes life possible.'

One might retort that the people may only be drowning sorrows of their own in their moments of gaiety, that in fact they are doing precisely what Tchaikovsky says he is doing himself in his annotation of the second movement, with the only difference that, instead of seeking escape in dreams, they find it in merriment; but it is indicative of his interest in his own affairs that he cannot admit the possibility of similar feelings in others, and in trying to interpret them musically, falls back on what is apparent on the surface. Here, surely, is an argument in defence of his egotism: had he continued to think only about himself to the end of the Symphony, he would unquestionably have written a better Finale.

40   *Orchestral Works of Tchaikovsky*

The music bursts at once with the utmost vigour into the exposition of this theme:

Ex. 32. *Allegro con fuoco.*

played in octave unison after an initial chord. (It should be noticed, incidentally, that the whole of the last movement departs from the minor key, being written in F major from the beginning.) This passage, though used a good deal in the course of the movement, is only a preamble to the principal subject, which is very soon introduced by the wood-wind:

Ex. 33. *Allegro.*

It is a Russian folk-tune, 'In the fields there stood a birch tree,' picturesquely scored with a broken *pizzicato* bass and snatches of scale passages derived from No. 32 running between the phrases. They lead back with a gradual *crescendo* to the return of the opening material, now prolonged and if possible noisier than before. Nor is the din diminished when the second subject appears in full orchestral trim:

Ex. 34.

Symphony No. 4, in F minor (Op. 36)

Its rather empty aggressiveness is somewhat redeemed by the not unoriginal modulatory passage that follows and the ringing triplet figures which lead to a full close.

The working-out now begins with the folk-song theme (No. 33), more quietly scored at first, but still accompanied by the agitated scales and soon lashed to a climax by violin tremolos and wood-wind chords repeated in triplets. It is then developed by diminution, imitation, and rhythmic distortion, but it never becomes a really pliable subject. With true peasant obstinacy it refuses to comply with symphonic etiquette; it remains angular and obtrusive, and will not be polished down to formal beauty or utility. All that Tchaikovsky can do is to proceed rapidly to the recapitulation, which is as vociferous as the exposition and more wearisome, because it verbally repeats statements that never appealed greatly to the hearer's mentality, but merely astonished him at first by a violent assault upon his nerves. Once again an attempt is made to extract significance from the main theme, and for a moment it looks as if, by means of a closer interweaving of its first phrase, it would succeed. But the effort is frittered away in yet another outbreak of brutal sonority.

But suddenly an astounding melodramatic effect is secured by a nerve-shattering return of the Fate theme

(No. 20) from the first movement, thundered out with the utmost force at first and then sinking down, with a resigned slackening, to a low moan. And now, to a drum roll that begins almost inaudibly and swells up by degrees, a surging climax is built up with a crude but exceedingly cunning mastery of stage-craft, on fragments of the second subject (No. 34). The final pages, chiefly based on Nos. 32 and 33, whenever the music is not pounding away at meaningless tonic-and-dominant cadenzas, are theatrical rodomontade of the most arrant order. The magniloquent orator wastes an immense amount of energy on the mere self-evident information that he is saying his last.

Suite from the Ballet 'Casse-Noisette' (Op. 71a)

Composed, February 1891—February 1892.
Orchestration: Piccolo, 3 Flutes, 2 Oboes, English Horn, 2 Clarinets, Bass Clarinet, 2 Bassoons, 4 Horns, 2 Trumpets, 3 Trombones, Tuba, Kettledrums, Triangle, Tambourine, Cymbals, Chimes, Celesta, Harp, and Strings.

1. Miniature Overture. 2. Six Characteristic Dances: (*a*) March; (*b*) Dance of the Sugar-Plum Fairy; (*c*) Trepak; (*d*) Arabian Dance; (*e*) Chinese Dance; (*f*) Reed-Pipe Dance. 3. Waltz of the Flowers.

In the space of thirteen years that fall between the fourth Symphony and the present work, Tchaikovsky had acquired universal fame and complete pecuniary independence. In 1887 he began a series of international tours which earned him brilliant successes everywhere, and the following year the Tsar granted him an annual pension of 3,000 roubles. It was in 1890 that Nadejda von Meck discontinued her allowance to him. Subject to a nervous disorder, she believed herself on the verge of bankruptcy, a fear she afterwards discovered to have been unfounded. Tchaikovsky was not unnaturally under the impression that her alarm had been feigned as an excuse to withdraw benefits which now looked to him like a passing whim; but it is not unlikely that the unfortunate breach with his benefactress was in some measure due to his consciousness that he ought to have declined this extra income as soon as the urgent need for it had passed.

In February 1891 the Imperial Opera at St. Petersburg commissioned Tchaikovsky to write a one-act Opera, 'Iolanthe,' after Herz's play, 'King René's Daughter,' and a Ballet on a scenario based on the fairytale of 'Nutcracker and Mouse-King' from E. T. A. Hoffmann's cycle of romantic stories, 'Die Serapions-Brüder'.

This is the plot of the Ballet, briefly told:

It is Christmas. The scene takes place in the home of an old-fashioned wealthy German family. The parents are seen adorning and lighting up an enormous Christmas tree. Guests arrive and the children are called in to receive their presents, among which is a comical little wooden man who turns out to be a Nutcracker. The children are delighted, but Fritz handles the toy so roughly that his little sister Claire is obliged to take it under her especial protection. Later on, when the children have been sent to bed, she returns in her nightgown to look after her favourite, but falls asleep amid her toys. An army of mice now appears and there is a tremendous battle between them and the tin soldiers, the former being led by their king and the latter by the Nutcracker. Claire in her dream sees with growing alarm that the mice are going to be victorious, and she throws her slipper at the Mouse-King, whereupon his subjects disappear and the Nutcracker is transformed into Prince Charming.

The second act takes place in the enchanted castle of Confiturembourg, where Claire's great deed is celebrated by festivities which provide ample excuse for a number of costume dances, several of which form part of the Suite.

Tchaikovsky began the work immediately, but it was interrupted by his departure for the U.S.A. in March 1891. He visited Paris on the way and gave a concert of his own works with the Colonne orchestra, retiring afterwards to Rouen, where he spent ten days at work on 'Iolanthe' and 'Casse-Noisette'. Just before he was due to embark at Havre he received news of the death of his sister, Alexandra Davidov, and he sailed to New York in a state of great despondency, feeling quite unable to give his mind to anything so frivolous as a Ballet. Even after his return to Russia in May, the work was continually interrupted by fits of depression. Then followed another concert tour abroad, which Tchaikovsky had to abandon owing to nostalgia and dejection that drove him back home before he could carry out his plan to visit Holland. It was not until February 1892 that he settled down in his country house at Maidanovo and finished the orchestration of those numbers of 'Casse-Noisette' which were to be given in the form of a Suite at a concert in St. Petersburg on 7/19 March. The whole Ballet was not performed until 5/17 December, when it was produced at the St. Petersburg Opera together with 'Iolanthe'.

I. In the *Miniature Overture* the composer at once makes it clear that we have to do with a children's tale and with toys, by discarding all the grown-up instruments of the orchestra. Its gruff-voiced, low-pitched members are all absent from the score. The only bass instruments that are used, the bassoons, are compelled to screw up their voices so as to keep mainly in the region of the tenor clef, and the horns, which can growl on occasions, speak rarely and discreetly. For percussion, the gentle triangle alone does service, and among the strings the violas have to supply the bass. Musical invention, too, is on a small scale here, as it is throughout the Suite, but it is highly fanciful and always enlivened by neat orchestral touches. The whole is featherweight music, of no more account in comparison with the supreme achievements of the art than a pretty picture-book is compared with great painting, but it is contrived with a sprightliness of imagination and a transparency of orchestration always perfectly proportionate to its minuteness.

The Overture begins *allegro giusto* with this trim little theme:

the re-statement of which with a new, busy semiquaver accompaniment at once illustrates Tchaikovsky's manner of enhancing his slender material by some deft touch or another (Ex. 36).

The music bustles on for a little while and then, after a humorous bridge-passage with explosive accents off the beat, comes a tune in the first violins, accompanied by syncopated *pizzicati* that keep up the quick

Ex. 36. Allegro.

pulse of the music which the rather oily new melody might otherwise tend to hinder:

This too is afterwards elaborated by means of new scoring. The music is then worked up brilliantly to the conclusion of the exposition. The customary working-out section is omitted and we proceed straight to the recapitulation, which is that of the normal sonata form, with the second subject (No. 37) in a different key. Ballet has no time to waste on structural ingenuities; its business is simply to entertain, and if it must have a formal Overture at all, the more swiftly it proceeds to the rise of the curtain, the better. The present example does this with brilliant precipitance in a tiny but strenuous *coda* admirably designed to awaken the spectator's curiosity.

II. There is no doubt that Tchaikovsky assembled the pick of the Ballet when he was asked to extract a Suite from it for concert performance. The *Six Charac-*

Suite from the Ballet 'Casse-Noisette'

teristic *Dances* will always remain ideal specimens of ballet music at its best. They appear in the middle of the Suite, tidily packed like a box of chocolates, all of a size and distinctly of the same make, all equally delicious, yet each with a flavour of its own. And there is next to no padding of paper shavings, of which, to tell the truth, the Ballet as a whole is stuffed very liberally full. Only those who know the complete work can tell how well the selection of the daintiest morsels was made, for it contains many passages with a plethora of notes that mean absolutely nothing and have no function but that of inflating the music to the required length. Much of 'Casse-Noisette' is musical upholstery of the worst kind.

(*a*) The use of the full orchestra, held in reserve until now makes its due effect in the *March*. But although pompous, this piece is not unduly so. It is clearly not a state function which is accompanied by this music, but only the gathering around a Christmas tree of an amiable German bourgeoisie dressed in the grotesque fashion of the Directoire period. The whole piece is evolved by the antithesis of short, contrasting phrases and humorously coloured by occasional crashing chords. The later addition of upward scales in the strings, downward arpeggios in the flute, and notes rapidly repeated in pairs by the bassoons, again show Tchaikovsky's deftness in keeping alive our interest by merely admixing a new colour element to phrases previously made familiar.

(*b*) In the Ballet the *Dance of the Sugar-Plum Fairy* is one of the variations of a *Pas de Deux* between Claire and the Nutcracker, this being a solo dance for the former. It is here that Tchaikovsky introduced the celesta, which he had heard in Paris in March 1891, for the first time into a Russian work. His use of a new means is remarkably successful. He reduces the orchestral sound to mere froth in order to match the instrument's slender notes. It is heard in limpidly tinkling figures over a delicate *pizzicato* harmony, and the bass clarinet, with its characteristic rotundity of tone, adds little downward-gliding phrases (afterwards taken up by the ordinary clarinets), which have a delicious effect of alternately shooting in and out of the musical texture, now protruding, now blending in. Another slight contrast is added for a moment in the shape of buzzing triplets in the violas. It should be noted how Tchaikovsky deliberately selects the dark colours of the orchestral palette (clarinets, violas) to set against the rather cloying celesta tone. The only passage where a ceremonious compliment to the newly-discovered instrument can be detected is a short unaccompanied arpeggio episode where it is left to captivate the ear alone. But it is given nothing of consequence to say, and seems therefore guilty of a curious lapse of taste, like an actor who suddenly forgets his part in the play and addresses the audience with a shallow remark of his own.

(*c*) The *Trepak*, though plainly in the manner of a Cossack dance, is Russian music with a cosmopolitan veneer, the kind of thing that made Tchaikovsky, for reasons of taste rather than by any real antipathy, the antagonist of the national school of which Balakirev was the leader and Borodin and Moussorgsky were the strongest exponents. It has nothing of the splendid primitive strength of these local geniuses, though nothing either, it must be conceded, of their occasional amateurishness. On the other hand, the technical facility which Tchaikovsky possessed in a superior degree was apt to run away with him at times and to impart a certain smugness to his music. This can be discerned in the *Trepak*, which remains decorous throughout in spite of its affectation of savagery. However, one must bear in mind that the Cossacks who perform this dance have no hot blood flowing in their veins, but are only filled with sawdust.

The use of the full orchestra, after the daintily scored preceding movement, is very telling, but Tchaikovsky overtaxes it a little. There is no point in using such characteristic instruments as English horn and bass clarinet in *tutti* passages going at full blast, where they add nothing to the orchestral colour and cannot be heard individually. Their tone does not stand out at any point of this movement, which proceeds in the conventional Cossack manner, growing louder and more animated towards the end.

(*d*) The *Arabian Dance* is performed in the Ballet by a character dressed according to the title and representing Coffee. (There is another dance preceding it, entitled Chocolate, in the nature of a Viennese Waltz, but this is not included in the Suite.) Drowsy Eastern languor is admirably suggested by melancholy figures for two clarinets and English horn, the latter placed in the middle of the three-part harmony, given out over a continuous drone bass of open fifths. Later, muted violins add another yearning phrase and the tambourine touches in the lightest strokes of local colour. The original thematic material is never abandoned, but presented in various new ways as the music proceeds. The piece is truly Oriental in its tenacious hugging of a single idea, but there is no attempt at ethnological accuracy. Just as in a children's picture-book a Western artist would draw an Eastern incident in the manner learnt in his own schools and based upon the conventions of his own people, so Tchaikovsky treats his little exotic pictures merely as an amused onlooker, adapting them to his own style for the delight of others.

(*e*) In the *Chinese Dance* again, the dancers, who represent Tea this time, are never for a moment depicted for us as real Chinamen. They simply affect a charmingly fantastic Chinese disguise for our entertainment. Tchaikovsky does not use the pentatonic scale, which is too often thought sufficient to make a piece appear authentically Chinese. There are rhythmic figures for piccolo and flutes, underlined here and there by chimes and alternating with syncopated passages for strings, which on a uniform rhythmic and harmonic surface have the effect of queer silhouettes detaching themselves sharply and in regular recurrence from a screen or wallpaper *à la chinoise*.

(*f*) The *Reed-Pipe Dance* too has a dainty artificiality, the kind of absurd unreality which all things assume behind the footlights at a Christmas pantomime. The pretty shapes traced by three flutes over a *pizzicato* background are unlike anything ever heard on a reed-pipe in the open air, but they capture the style of a charmingly conventionalized theatrical show to perfection. The rather greasy tune contributed by the English horn has the same quality of attractively coloured pasteboard, and the elaborations of the main theme by the strings a moment later are so many applications of tinsel made by a master of stage effect. Then comes, introduced by brass and percussion, an episode of mock rusticity, followed by a brief re-statement of the earlier material.

III. Although so far Tchaikovsky has shown great discernment in selecting the best numbers of the

Suite from the Ballet 'Casse-Noisette'

'Casse-Noisette' score for his Suite, he finishes with an example where his ballet music is seen at its tawdriest. The *Waltz of the Flowers* skirts vulgarity so closely that the critics who accuse it of actual trespass have little difficulty in proving their case. The use of gold-leaf and glittering gauze here certainly passes the borders of good taste, and it is only in a kind of amused indulgence granted to a rather old-fashioned and gaudy stage entertainment that one tolerates the blatancy of this piece. The harp cadenza in the introduction is a specimen of the worst pages in the ballet music, an ornament the elaborateness of which, empty and unlovely in itself, stands in no just proportion to its utility. The rest is ballroom music, not without liveliness, but quite devoid of elegance. It is a dance, not of flowers, but of very matter-of-fact youths and maidens, watched over by voluminous duennas and experienced matrons with dishonourable matrimonial intentions. At the final climax the music swirls into a vortex of actual and figurative loudness.

ST. MARY'S COLLEGE OF MARYLAND
ST. MARY'S CITY, MARYLAND

THE LIBRARY
ST. MARY'S COLLEGE OF MARYLAND
ST. MARY'S CITY, MARYLAND 20686